The Book of Puns

Published by Willow Creek Press, Inc.
P.O. Box 147, Minocqua, Wisconsin 54548

Printed in Canada

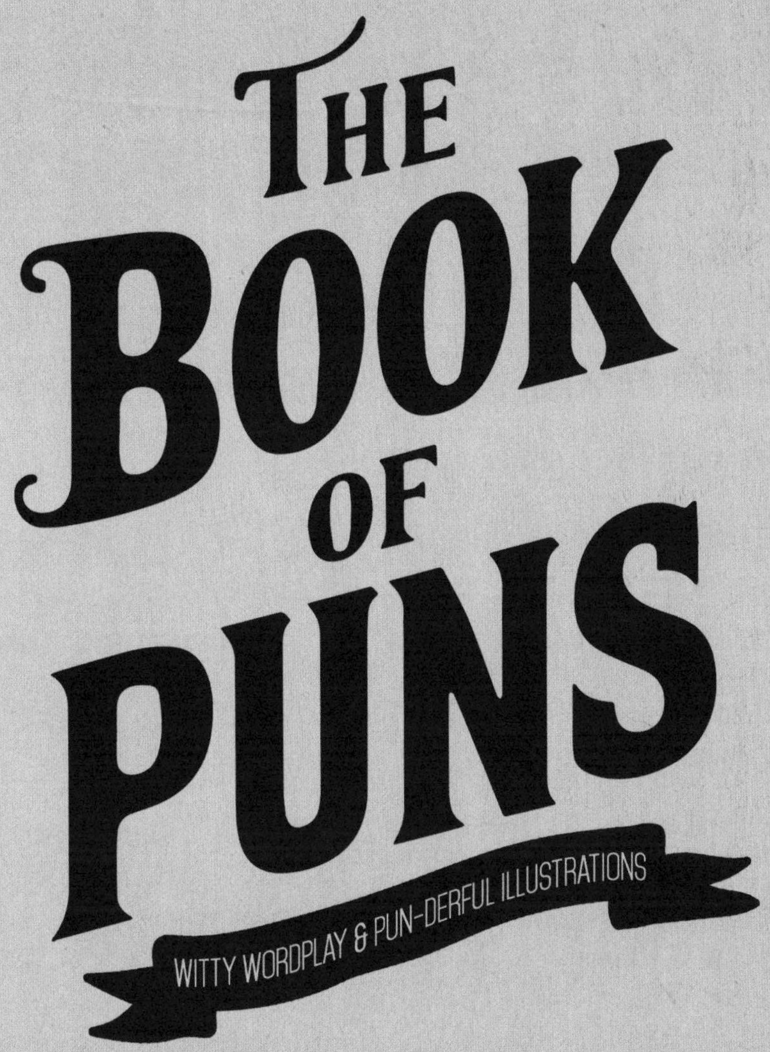

WILLOW CREEK PRESS®

I DID A THEATRICAL PERFORMANCE ABOUT PUNS.
REALLY IT WAS JUST A PLAY ON WORDS.

THINGS MADE IN AUSTRALIA ARE HIGH KOALA-TY.

WHENEVER I FEEL BLUE, I START BREATHING AGAIN.

WHEN MY ICE HOUSE FALLS APART
IGLOO IT BACK TOGETHER.

MY WIFE LIKES IT WHEN I BLOW AIR ON HER
WHEN SHE'S HOT, BUT HONESTLY... I'M NOT A FAN.

HAPPINESS IS WHEN
YOU'RE RIGHT BESIDE ME.

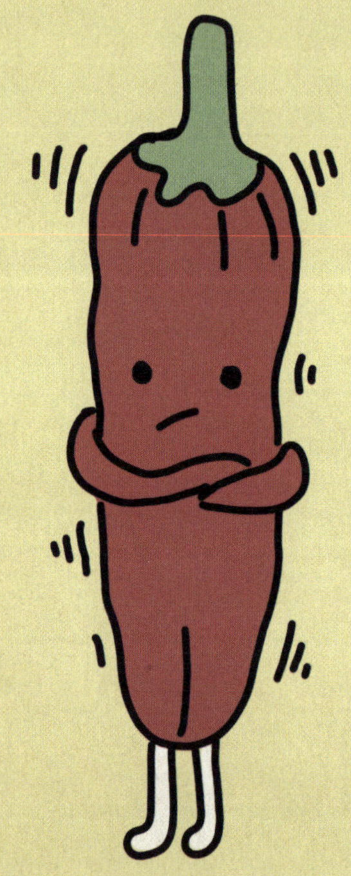

I'M A LITTLE CHILI.

JUSTICE IS A DISH BEST SERVED COLD BECAUSE IF IT WERE SERVED WARM, IT WOULD BE JUST WATER.

I ALWAYS WANTED TO LEARN TO PROCRASTINATE... JUST NEVER GOT AROUND TO IT.

WENT TO QUITE A FEW STORES TO FIND THE BEST PRICES FOR HERBS... I THINK IT WAS THYME WELL SPENT.

FIXING BROKEN WINDOWS IS A PANE IN THE GLASS.

THERE WAS A BIG PADDLE SALE AT THE BOAT STORE. IT WAS QUITE AN OAR DEAL.

I UNDERSTAND HOW GEMS ARE MADE. THE CONCEPT IS CRYSTAL CLEAR TO ME.

IT WAS COLD IN THE BEDROOM SO I LAID DOWN IN THE FIREPLACE AND SLEPT LIKE A LOG.

I GAVE ALL MY DEAD BATTERIES AWAY... THEY WERE FREE OF CHARGE!

I COULDN'T WORK OUT HOW TO FASTEN MY SEATBELT FOR AGES. BUT THEN ONE DAY, IT JUST CLICKED.

REFUSING TO GO TO THE GYM COUNTS AS RESISTANCE TRAINING, RIGHT?

I'M SEW INTO YOU!

I'M FEELING LIGHTHEADED.

I'VE ACCIDENTALLY SWALLOWED SOME SCRABBLE TILES. MY NEXT POOP COULD SPELL DISASTER.

THERE WAS A RECENT STUDY THAT TRIED TO PINPOINT THE EFFECT THAT ALCOHOL HAD ON WALKING. THE RESULT WAS STAGGERING.

IF YOU JUMPED OFF A BRIDGE IN PARIS, YOU'D BE IN SEINE.

I'VE BEEN LEARNING BRAILLE. I'M SURE I'LL MASTER IT ONCE I GET A FEEL FOR IT.

A RUBBER BAND PISTOL WAS CONFISCATED FROM ALGEBRA CLASS, BECAUSE IT WAS A WEAPON OF MATH DISRUPTION.

SHE WAS ONLY A WHISKEY MAKER, BUT I LOVED HER STILL.

I PLANNED TO FIND MY WATCH TODAY, BUT I DIDN'T HAVE THE TIME.

I'M WORKING ON A DEVICE THAT WILL READ MINDS. I'D LOVE TO HEAR YOUR THOUGHTS.

NEVER LIE TO AN X-RAY TECHNICIAN. THEY CAN SEE RIGHT THROUGH YOU.

SUE BROKE HER FINGER TODAY, BUT ON THE OTHER HAND SHE WAS COMPLETELY FINE.

I FEEL A STRONG
CONNECTION
WITH YOU.

LET'S HANG OUT.

I RECENTLY GOT CRUSHED BY A PILE OF BOOKS, BUT I SUPPOSE I'VE ONLY GOT MY SHELF TO BLAME.

WHAT IS A HURRICANE'S FAVORITE GAME?
TWISTER.

MY TENNIS OPPONENT WAS NOT TOO HAPPY WITH MY SERVES, HE KEPT RETURNING THEM.

MASKS HAVE NO FACE VALUE.

I WENT TO A BUFFET DINNER WITH MY NEIGHBOR, WHO IS A TAXIDERMIST. AFTER SUCH A BIG MEAL, I WAS STUFFED.

SKUNKS LOVE VALENTINE'S DAY BECAUSE THEY ARE VERY SCENT-IMENTAL.

I'VE DECIDED TO SELL MY VACUUM... IT WAS JUST COLLECTING DUST.

I FOUND A ROCK YESTERDAY WHICH MEASURED 1,760 YARDS IN LENGTH. MUST BE SOME KIND OF MILESTONE.

ZEBRAS ARE JUST HORSES THAT ESCAPED FROM PRISON.

MY SISTER WAS CRYING SO I ASKED HER IF SHE WAS HAVING A CRY-SIS.

ALOE, HOW
ARE YOU?

LONG THYME
NO SEE.

YOU SPICE UP
MY LIFE.

I APPLIED FOR A JOB IN A HEALTH CLUB, BUT THEY SAID I WASN'T FIT FOR THE JOB.

THIS MORNING SOME CLOWN OPENED THE DOOR FOR ME. I THOUGHT TO MYSELF THAT'S A NICE JESTER.

I RAN OUT OF POKER CHIPS SO I USED DRIED FRUITS FOR PLAYING INSTEAD. PEOPLE WENT NUTS WHEN THEY SAW ME RAISIN THE STAKES.

I'M GLAD I KNOW SIGN LANGUAGE, IT'S PRETTY HANDY.

CLAUSTROPHOBIC PEOPLE ARE MORE PRODUCTIVE THINKING OUT OF THE BOX.

I THOUGHT ABOUT GOING ON AN ALL-ALMOND DIET. BUT THAT'S JUST NUTS!

GETTING PAID TO SLEEP WOULD BE A DREAM JOB.

THE TIME MACHINE AND I GO WAY BACK.

A MUSHROOM WALKS INTO A BAR AND ORDERS A DRINK. THE BARTENDER TELLS HIM TO GET OUT. THE MUSHROOM SAYS, "WHY? I'M A FUN-GUY."

I USED TO BE A BAKER, BUT I DIDN'T MAKE ENOUGH DOUGH.

COUCH POTATO

STAY POSITIVE.

REGULAR VISITORS TO THE DENTIST ARE FAMILIAR WITH THE DRILL.

ACUPUNCTURE IS A JAB WELL DONE.

I DON'T WANT TO CUT MY HAIR! I'M REALLY ATTACHED TO IT.

THIS GRAVITY JOKE IS GETTING A BIT OLD, BUT I FALL FOR IT EVERY TIME.

AFTER MANUALLY ROTATING THE HEAVY MACHINERY, THE WORKER GREW PRETTY CRANKY.

WITH GREAT REFLEXES COMES GREAT RESPONSE ABILITY.

I MANAGED TO GET A GOOD JOB FOR A POOL MAINTENANCE COMPANY, BUT THE WORK WAS JUST TOO DRAINING.

AS A WIZARD, I ENJOY TURNING OBJECTS INTO GLASS. JUST WANTED TO MAKE THAT CLEAR.

I WANNA MAKE A JOKE ABOUT SODIUM, BUT NA...

TODAY AT THE BANK, AN OLD LADY ASKED ME TO HELP CHECK HER BALANCE... SO I PUSHED HER OVER.

I'M SO ATTRACTED TO YOU.

SPREAD HAP-PEA-NESS.

A PAIR OF JUMPER CABLES WALK INTO A BAR AND ASK FOR A DRINK. THE BARTENDER SAYS, "OK, BUT I DON'T WANT YOU STARTING ANYTHING IN HERE."

THE PILOT WAS A LONER BUT EVEN FOR HIM FLYING A DRONE WAS SIMPLY TOO REMOTE.

I SAW A DOCUMENTARY ON HOW SHIPS ARE KEPT TOGETHER. IT WAS RIVETING!

I GET DISTRACTED BY ALL THE MEATS IN THE DELI SECTION, MUST BE MY SHORT ATTENTION SPAM.

TREE TRIMMERS DO SUCH A FANTASTIC JOB, THEY SHOULD TAKE A BOUGH.

BRITAIN WAS A WET PLACE DUE TO THE QUEEN'S LONG REIGN.

A BOILED EGG IN THE MORNING IS HARD TO BEAT.

GOATS IN FRANCE ARE GREAT MUSICIANS BECAUSE THEY HAVE FRENCH HORNS.

POLICE HAVE ARRESTED THE WORLD TONGUE-TWISTER CHAMPION. I IMAGINE HE'LL BE GIVEN A TOUGH SENTENCE.

A LAWYER-TURNED-COOK IS A SUE CHEF.

WE WERE WATER
BEFORE IT
WAS COOL

WE'VE GOT CHEMISTRY.

NEED AN ARK?
I NOAH GUY.

MY WIFE WARNED ME NOT TO STEAL THE KITCHEN UTENSILS, BUT IT'S A WHISK I'M WILLING TO TAKE.

I WASN'T ORIGINALLY GOING TO GET A BRAIN TRANSPLANT, BUT THEN I CHANGED MY MIND.

DON'T SPELL PART BACKWARDS. IT'S A TRAP.

THIEVES HAD BROKEN INTO MY HOUSE AND STOLEN EVERYTHING EXCEPT MY SOAP, SHOWER GEL, TOWELS AND DEODORANT. DIRTY HOOLIGANS.

I'VE JUST WRITTEN A SONG ABOUT TORTILLAS.
ACTUALLY, IT'S MORE OF A RAP.

LAST TIME I GOT CAUGHT STEALING
A CALENDAR I GOT 12 MONTHS.

MY COMPUTER'S GOT MILEY VIRUS.
IT HAS STOPPED TWERKING.

I'M READING A BOOK ABOUT ANTI-GRAVITY.
IT'S IMPOSSIBLE TO PUT DOWN.

I COULDN'T QUITE REMEMBER HOW TO THROW A
BOOMERANG, BUT EVENTUALLY, IT CAME BACK TO ME.

I'M SO BOARD.

THANK YOU
FOR KEEPING
ME TOGETHER.

I DECIDED TO BECOME A PROFESSIONAL FISHERMAN, BUT DISCOVERED THAT I COULDN'T LIVE ON MY NET INCOME.

ABOUT A MONTH BEFORE HE DIED, MY UNCLE HAD HIS BACK COVERED IN LARD. AFTER THAT, HE WENT DOWN HILL FAST.

THE CARPENTER CAME AROUND THE OTHER DAY. HE MADE THE BEST ENTRANCE I HAVE EVER SEEN...

OLD ARTISTS NEVER RETIRE, THEY WITHDRAW INSTEAD!

A MAN KNOCKED ON MY DOOR AND ASKED FOR A SMALL DONATION FOR A LOCAL SWIMMING POOL. SO I GAVE HIM A GLASS OF WATER.

I WAS GOING TO TELL MY PIZZA JOKE
BUT I THINK IT'S A BIT TOO CHEESY.

THE NEWSPAPER'S RATIONALE FOR RUNNING
THE STORY WAS PAPER THIN.

I SAW AN ADVERTISEMENT THAT READ: "TELEVISION
FOR SALE, $1, VOLUME STUCK ON FULL."
I THOUGHT TO MYSELF, I CAN'T TURN THAT DOWN.

IF A SHORT PSYCHIC BROKE OUT OF JAIL, THEN
YOU'D HAVE A SMALL MEDIUM AT LARGE.

I'D LOVE TO VISIT HOLLAND, WOODEN SHOE?

I'M HOTTER
I'M COOLER

TOUGH COOKIE

IF THE RIGHT SIDE OF THE BRAIN CONTROLS THE LEFT SIDE OF THE BODY, THEN LEFTIES ARE THE ONLY ONES IN THEIR RIGHT MIND.

THE CARDIOVASCULAR SYSTEM IS A WORK OF ARTERY, BUT IT IS ALSO PRETTY VEIN.

I USED TO BE ADDICTED TO SOAP, BUT I'M CLEAN NOW.

CLEANING MIRRORS IS A JOB I COULD REALLY SEE MYSELF DOING.

I HATE RUSSIAN DOLLS, THEY'RE SO FULL OF THEMSELVES.

DID YOU HEAR ABOUT THE GUY WHO GOT HIT IN THE HEAD WITH A CAN OF SODA?
HE WAS LUCKY IT WAS A SOFT DRINK.

MY GIRLFRIEND TOLD ME SHE WAS LEAVING ME BECAUSE I KEEP PRETENDING TO BE A TRANSFORMER. I SAID, "NO, WAIT! I CAN CHANGE."

I TRIED TO CATCH SOME FOG, I MIST.

IF YOU EVER GET COLD, JUST STAND IN A CORNER FOR A BIT...
THEY'RE USUALLY AROUND 90 DEGREES.

CAN FEBRUARY MARCH? NO, BUT APRIL MAY!

HOW WAS YOUR DATE?
GREAT, WE JUST CLICKED.

SORRY, YOU'RE JUST NOT MY TYPE.

I SAW AN AD FOR BURIAL PLOTS, AND THOUGHT TO MYSELF THIS IS THE LAST THING I NEED.

WHEN I GET NAKED IN THE BATHROOM, THE SHOWER USUALLY GETS TURNED ON.

A BICYCLE CAN'T STAND ON ITS OWN BECAUSE IT'S TWO TIRED.

TO WRITE WITH A BROKEN PENCIL IS POINTLESS.

THE LIBRARIAN DIDN'T KNOW WHAT TO DO WITH THE BOOK ABOUT TESLA'S LOVE OF ELECTRICITY, SO HE FILED IT UNDER "CURRENT AFFAIRS."

IF A CHILD REFUSES TO SLEEP DURING NAP TIME, ARE THEY GUILTY OF RESISTING A REST?

TWO WINDMILLS ARE STANDING IN A FIELD AND ONE ASKS THE OTHER, "WHAT KIND OF MUSIC DO YOU LIKE?" THE OTHER SAYS, "I'M A BIG METAL FAN."

ENGLAND DOESN'T HAVE A KIDNEY BANK, BUT IT DOES HAVE A LIVERPOOL.

I WONDERED WHY THE BASEBALL WAS GETTING BIGGER. THEN IT HIT ME.

TODAY I MET THE VEGETARIAN BROTHER OF BRUCE LEE. BROCCO LEE.

YOU COMPLETE ME.

I'LL BE WATCHING YOU.

LAST WEEK I CALLED SOMEONE A WATERING HOLE BUT I MEANT WELL.

TOILET PAPER PLAYS AN IMPORTANT ROLL IN MY LIFE.

I USED TO HATE MATH UNTIL I REALIZED THAT DECIMALS HAVE A POINT.

MY FRIEND ASKED ME HOW I BAKE MY BREAD. I SAID I COULDN'T TELL HIM BECAUSE IT WAS ON A KNEAD TO KNOW BASIS.

CORDUROY PILLOWS ARE MAKING HEADLINES.

I GOT A NEW PAIR OF GLOVES TODAY, BUT THEY'RE BOTH "LEFTS" WHICH, ON THE ONE HAND, IS GREAT, BUT ON THE OTHER, IT'S JUST NOT RIGHT.

AS A SCARECROW, PEOPLE SAY I'M OUTSTANDING IN MY FIELD. BUT HAY, IT'S IN MY JEANS.

MY BOSS IS GOING TO FIRE THE EMPLOYEE WITH THE WORST POSTURE. I HAVE A HUNCH, IT MIGHT BE ME.

I'M TAKING PART IN A STAIR CLIMBING COMPETITION. GUESS I BETTER STEP UP MY GAME.

I WAS ADDICTED TO THE HOKEY POKEY... BUT THANKFULLY, I TURNED MYSELF AROUND.

YOU'RE SO BREW-TIFUL
AWW, I DONUT KNOW WHAT I'D DO WITHOUT YOU.

CHILL PILL

SOMETIMES I TUCK MY KNEES INTO MY CHEST AND LEAN FORWARD. THAT'S JUST HOW I ROLL.

PIG PUNS ARE REALLY BOARING.

"DOCTOR, THERE'S A PATIENT ON LINE 1 THAT SAYS HE'S INVISIBLE."
"WELL, TELL HIM I CAN'T SEE HIM RIGHT NOW."

A COURTROOM ARTIST WAS ARRESTED TODAY FOR AN UNKNOWN REASON... DETAILS ARE SKETCHY.

WAKING UP IN THE MORNING IS AN EYE-OPENING EXPERIENCE.

DON'T TRUST ATOMS, THEY MAKE UP EVERYTHING.

DOES MY BRAND-NEW SMILE DENTURE EGO?

THE RACE CAR DRIVER HAD A PRETTY CHECKERED PAST...

I WAITED AND STAYED UP ALL NIGHT TO FIGURE OUT WHERE THE SUN GOES. THEN IT DAWNED ON ME.

HACKERS BROUGHT DOWN MY ONLINE BUSINESS BUT I MANAGED TO KEEP THE WEBSITE ADDRESS AND THAT'S DOMAIN THING.

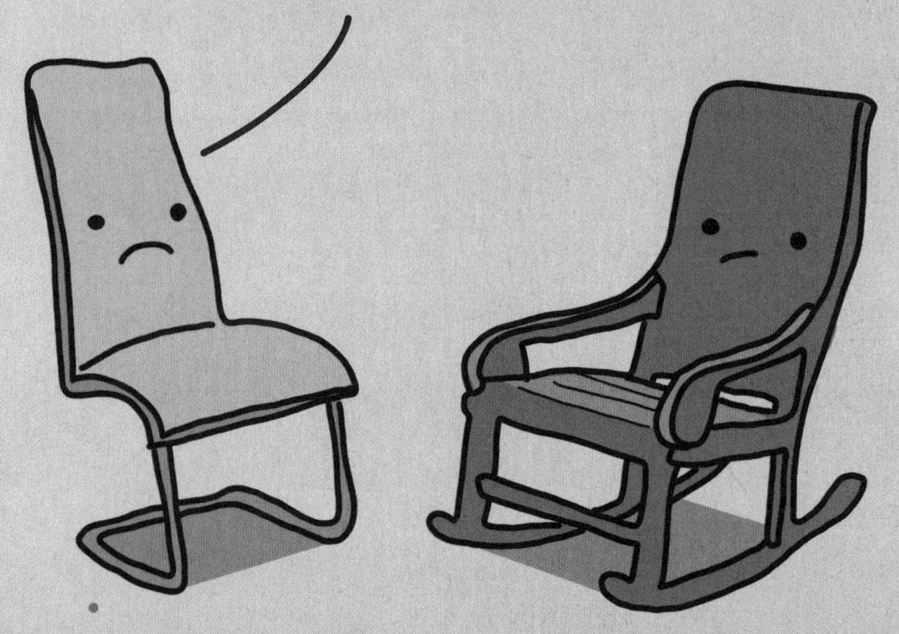
EVERYONE SAYS I
LOOK UNSTABLE!

LET THE BEET DROP.

I BOUGHT THE WORLD'S WORST THESAURUS YESTERDAY. NOT ONLY IS IT TERRIBLE, IT'S TERRIBLE.

I TRIED TO SUE THE AIRLINE FOR LOSING MY LUGGAGE. I LOST MY CASE.

I CAN CUT WOOD BY JUST LOOKING AT IT. IT'S TRUE! I SAW IT WITH MY OWN EYES.

WHEN A CLOCK IS STILL HUNGRY, IT GOES BACK FOUR SECONDS.

I COULDN'T BELIEVE THAT THE HIGHWAY DEPARTMENT CALLED MY DAD A THIEF BUT WHEN I GOT HOME, ALL THE SIGNS WERE THERE.

I'VE GOT A CHICKEN-PROOF GARDEN.
IT'S COMPLETELY IMPECCABLE!

TWO LOAVES OF BREAD WANTED TO GET MARRIED, WHICH IS WHY THEY ELOAFED.

THE WEIGH-IN AT THE SUMO WRESTLING CHAMPIONSHIP WAS A LARGE SCALE EFFORT.

I DIDN'T USE TO LIKE DUCT-TAPE AT FIRST, BUT I SOON BECAME ATTACHED TO IT.

I REMEMBER BEING IN SO MUCH DEBT THAT I COULDN'T AFFORD MY ELECTRICITY BILLS, IT WAS A DARK TIME.

I HAVE A HARD TIME
OPENING UP TO PEOPLE.

I'M COOLER THAN YOU.

A HAIR-RAISING EXPERIENCE SOUNDS PROMISING TO A BALD MAN.

NEVER DATE A TENNIS PLAYER. LOVE MEANS NOTHING TO THEM.

I'M NOT A HUGE FAN OF ARCHERY. IT HAS WAY TOO MANY DRAWBACKS!

I LIFT WEIGHTS ONLY ON SATURDAY AND SUNDAY BECAUSE MONDAY TO FRIDAY ARE WEAK DAYS.

THE PHARAOHS OF EGYPT CAME UP WITH THE FIRST PYRAMID SCHEME.

KIDS WHO DON'T LEARN TO TIE THEIR SHOES PROPERLY ARE BOUND TO WIND UP ON THE KNOTTY LIST.

I WAS GOING TO BUY A BOOK ON PHOBIAS, BUT I WAS AFRAID IT WOULDN'T HELP ME.

YOU CAN'T PLAY CARDS ON A SMALL BOAT BECAUSE SOMEONE IS ALWAYS HITTING THE DECK.

I CAN'T BELIEVE I GOT FIRED FROM THE CALENDAR FACTORY. ALL I DID WAS TAKE A DAY OFF.

AFTER A LONG TIME WAITING FOR THE BOWLING ALLEY TO OPEN, WE EVENTUALLY GOT THE BALL ROLLING.

TOGETHER WE BAKE
THINGS HAPPEN.

YOU ARE LOOKING
A LITTLE PAIL

I WORKED IN THE WOODS AS A LUMBERJACK, BUT I JUST COULDN'T HACK IT, SO THEY GAVE ME THE AX.

MY FRIEND'S BAKERY BURNED DOWN LAST NIGHT. NOW HIS BUSINESS IS TOAST.

A PET STORE HAD A BIRD CONTEST WITH NO PERCHES NECESSARY.

SOMEONE RIPPED SOME PAGES OUT OF BOTH ENDS OF MY DICTIONARY TODAY. IT JUST GOES FROM BAD TO WORSE!

MY NEW GIRLFRIEND WORKS AT THE ZOO. I THINK SHE IS A KEEPER.

I LOVE SWITZERLAND! I'M NOT SURE WHAT THE BEST THING ABOUT IT IS, BUT THEIR FLAG IS A BIG PLUS.

I BURNT MY HAWAIIAN PIZZA TODAY. I THINK I SHOULD HAVE COOKED IT ON ALOHA TEMPERATURE.

TWO CHEESE TRUCKS RAN INTO EACH OTHER. DE BRIE WAS EVERYWHERE.

PEOPLE WHO LACK THE PATIENCE FOR CALLIGRAPHY WILL NEVER HAVE PROPERLY FORMED CHARACTERS.

I LEFT MY LAST BOYFRIEND BECAUSE HE WOULDN'T STOP COUNTING. I WONDER WHAT HE'S UP TO NOW.

THE ANSWERS YOU ARE
LOOKING FOR ARE INSIDE YOU.

I'M LOST WITHOUT YOU.

JOKES ABOUT GERMAN SAUSAGE ARE THE WURST.

FISHERMEN ARE REEL MEN.

MY GRANDMA IS HAVING TROUBLE WITH HER NEW STAIR LIFT. IT'S DRIVING HER UP THE WALL.

I QUIT GYMNASTICS BECAUSE I WAS FED UP WITH HANGING AROUND THE BARS.

I'VE JUST BEEN ON A ONCE-IN-A-LIFETIME HOLIDAY. I'LL TELL YOU WHAT, NEVER AGAIN.

I WANTED TO TELL YOU A JOKE ABOUT LEECHES, BUT THEY ALL SUCK.

MY DOG MINTON ATE ALL MY SHUTTLECOCKS. BAD MINTON!

IT'S A LENGTHY ARTICLE ON JAPANESE SWORD FIGHTERS BUT I CAN SAMURAIS IT FOR YOU.

HAVE YOU EVER TRIED TO EAT A CLOCK? IT'S VERY TIME-CONSUMING.

IF SATAN EVER LOST HIS HAIR, THERE WOULD BE HELL TOUPEE.

NO PAIN,
NO GAIN.

BLIND DATE

A SMALL BOY SWALLOWED SOME COINS AND WAS TAKEN TO THE HOSPITAL. WHEN HIS GRANDMOTHER TELEPHONED TO ASK HOW HE WAS, THE NURSE SAID "NO CHANGE YET."

TO THE GUY WHO INVENTED ZERO: THANKS FOR NOTHING!

WHEN THE CANNIBAL SHOWED UP LATE FOR LUNCH, THE OTHERS GAVE HIM THE COLD SHOULDER.

I WOULDN'T BUY ANYTHING WITH VELCRO. IT'S A TOTAL RIP-OFF.

READING WHILE SUNBATHING MAKES YOU WELL RED.

I HAVE A SPEED BUMP PHOBIA BUT I'M SLOWLY GETTING OVER IT.

SOMEONE STOLE MY MOOD RING. I'M NOT SURE HOW I FEEL ABOUT THAT.

WHITE BOARDS ARE REMARKABLE.

I WENT TO A SEAFOOD DISCO LAST WEEK AND PULLED A MUSSEL.

I GOT THROWN OUT OF MATH CLASS FOR ONE TOO MANY INFRACTIONS.

DON'T STOP, KEEP GOING!

YOU CAN ALWAYS COUNT ON ME.

WHEN MAKING BUTTER THERE IS LITTLE MARGARINE FOR ERROR.

SINGING IN THE SHOWER IS ALL FUN AND GAMES UNTIL YOU GET SHAMPOO IN YOUR MOUTH. THEN IT BECOMES A SOAP OPERA.

MOST PEOPLE ARE SHOCKED WHEN THEY FIND OUT HOW BAD I AM AS AN ELECTRICIAN.

IT'S HARD TO EXPLAIN PUNS TO KLEPTOMANIACS BECAUSE THEY ALWAYS TAKE THINGS LITERALLY.

LEARNING HOW TO COLLECT TRASH WASN'T THAT HARD. I JUST PICKED IT UP AS I WENT ALONG.

SOMEONE THREW CHEESE AT ME. REAL MATURE!

I USED TO BE A TRAIN DRIVER
BUT I GOT SIDETRACKED.

YESTERDAY I ACCIDENTALLY SWALLOWED
SOME FOOD COLORING.
THE DOCTOR SAYS I'M OK, BUT I FEEL
LIKE I'VE DYED A LITTLE INSIDE.

WHEN I FINALLY WORKED OUT THE SECRET
TO CLONING, I WAS BESIDE MYSELF.

I WAS HAPPY WITH MY HISTORIAN JOB UNTIL
I REALIZED THERE WAS NO FUTURE IN IT.

LOOK, YOU'RE
BOTH NUTS!

I SEE A LOT OF MYSELF IN YOU.

I WENT TO A REALLY EMOTIONAL WEDDING THE OTHER DAY. EVEN THE CAKE WAS IN TIERS.

A MAN JUST ASSAULTED ME WITH MILK, CREAM AND BUTTER. HOW DAIRY.

I USED TO HAVE A FEAR OF HURDLES, BUT I GOT OVER IT.

IF A JUDGE LOVES THE SOUND OF HIS OWN VOICE, EXPECT A LONG SENTENCE.

A SIGN ON THE LAWN AT A DRUG REHAB CENTER SAID, "KEEP OFF THE GRASS."

A GOLF BALL IS A GOLF BALL NO MATTER HOW YOU PUTT IT.

MY FRIEND MADE A JOKE ABOUT A TV CONTROLLER. IT WASN'T REMOTELY FUNNY.

I THOUGHT I SAW AN EYE DOCTOR ON AN ALASKAN ISLAND, BUT IT TURNED OUT TO BE AN OPTICAL ALEUTIAN.

BROKEN PUPPETS FOR SALE. NO STRINGS ATTACHED.

MY SISTER BET ME $100 THAT I COULDN'T BUILD A WORKING CAR OUT OF SPAGHETTI. YOU SHOULD'VE SEEN HER FACE AS I DROVE PASTA.

I'M HALF EMPTY.
YOU NEED TO BE MORE POSITIVE.
O-
O+

I KNOW IT'S CORNY BUT
I THINK I LIKE YOU.

I CAN HEAR MUSIC COMING OUT FROM MY PRINTER. I THINK THE PAPER'S JAMMIN' AGAIN...

I RECENTLY HEARD ABOUT A MANNEQUIN THAT LOST ALL OF HIS FRIENDS BECAUSE HE WAS SO CLOTHES MINDED!

MY CEILING ISN'T THE BEST... BUT IT'S UP THERE!

WANNA GO ON A PICNIC? ALPACA LUNCH.

I WORK IN A PAPER FACTORY, WHERE MY RESPONSIBILITIES ARE TWOFOLD.

THEY'RE BUILDING A RESTAURANT ON MARS NOW. THEY SAY THE FOOD WILL BE GREAT, BUT THEY'RE WORRIED ABOUT THE LACK OF ATMOSPHERE.

NO MATTER HOW MUCH YOU PUSH THE ENVELOPE, IT'LL STILL BE STATIONERY.

IF LIFE GIVES YOU MELONS...
YOU MIGHT BE DYSLEXIC.

I WAS GOING TO SHARE A VEGETABLE JOKE BUT IT'S TOO CORNY.

I NEED TO STOP DRINKING SO MUCH MILK. IT'S AN UDDER DISGRACE.

I'M SINGLE.
ME TOO!

YOU ROCK.
YOU RULE.

TELLING A DEMOLITIONIST HOW TO DO HIS JOB IS DESTRUCTIVE CRITICISM.

I ACCIDENTALLY WENT TO BED WITH MY CONTACT LENSES IN THE OTHER NIGHT. MY DREAMS HAVE NEVER BEEN CLEARER.

A LOT OF PEOPLE CRY WHEN THEY CUT ONIONS. THE TRICK IS NOT TO FORM AN EMOTIONAL BOND.

I HAD A NECK BRACE FITTED YEARS AGO AND I'VE NEVER LOOKED BACK SINCE.

MY FIRST JOB WAS WORKING IN AN ORANGE JUICE FACTORY, BUT I GOT CANNED: COULDN'T CONCENTRATE.

I RELISH THE FACT THAT YOU'VE MUSTARD THE STRENGTH TO KETCHUP TO ME.

HUNG A PICTURE UP ON THE WALL THE OTHER DAY. NAILED IT.

A TERMITE WALKS INTO A BAR AND SAYS, "WHERE IS THE BAR TENDER?"

IF A DOG WAS A COMPUTER, WOULD ITS BARK BE BIGGER THAN ITS BYTE?

A PLATEAU IS THE HIGHEST FORM OF FLATTERY.

COME TO THE DARK SIDE.
TEA

YOU'RE SOY AMAZING.

I WENT TO SEE THE LIBERTY BELL THE OTHER DAY. IT'S NOT ALL IT'S CRACKED UP TO BE.

MY MOM JUST FOUND OUT THAT I'VE REPLACED HER BED WITH A TRAMPOLINE. SHE HIT THE ROOF.

MY SISTER WAS ENGAGED TO A MAN WITH A WOODEN LEG BUT SHE BROKE IT OFF.

DID YOU HEAR THE JOKE ABOUT THE PEANUT BUTTER? I'M NOT TELLING YOU. YOU MIGHT SPREAD IT!

ONCE YOU CONTRACT AN INFECTION OF THE BLADDER, URINE TROUBLE.

MY FRIEND ASKED ME TO SHIP HIM A TRUCKLOAD OF FOOD BUT IT JUST WASN'T PALATABLE.

SANG THE RAINBOW SONG IN FRONT OF A POLICE OFFICER, GOT ARRESTED FOR COLORFUL LANGUAGE.

I'D LOVE TO KNOW HOW THE EARTH ROTATES. IT WOULD TOTALLY MAKE MY DAY.

SOMEONE STOLE ALL MY LAMPS. I COULDN'T BE MORE DELIGHTED.

I ACCIDENTALLY SHOT SOMEONE WITH A STARTING GUN THE OTHER DAY. I'VE BEEN CHARGED WITH A RACE CRIME.

I'M KINDA
A BIG DILL.

DON'T WORRY. I GOT YOU COVERED.

I'D TELL YOU MY CONSTRUCTION JOKE
BUT I'M STILL WORKING ON IT.

I TOLD MY GIRLFRIEND SHE DREW HER EYEBROWS
TOO HIGH... SHE SEEMED SURPRISED.

I GOOGLED, "HOW TO START A CAMPFIRE."
I GOT 49,000 MATCHES.

WHEN MY GIRLFRIEND ASKED ME TO
STOP IMPERSONATING A FLAMINGO,
I HAD TO PUT MY FOOT DOWN.

I DON'T TRUST STAIRS. THEY'RE
ALWAYS UP TO SOMETHING.

THE GIRL QUIT HER JOB AT THE DONUT FACTORY BECAUSE SHE WAS FED UP WITH THE HOLE BUSINESS.

THE ARTIST THOUGHT HIS FAVORITE PAINT HAD BEEN STOLEN, BUT IT WAS JUST A PIGMENT OF HIS IMAGINATION.

DID YOU HEAR ABOUT THE KIDNAPPING AT SCHOOL? IT'S OKAY. HE WOKE UP.

TWO PEANUTS ARE WALKING DOWN THE STREET. ONE IS ASSAULTED.

COFFEE IS THE SILENT VICTIM IN OUR HOUSE. IT GETS MUGGED EVERY DAY.

LOOKS LIKE YOU'RE
NEW HERE?

YOU'RE MY
BUTTER HALF.

WHY SHOULDN'T YOU GOSSIP IN A CORN FIELD?
TOO MANY EARS AROUND.

6:30 IS THE BEST TIME ON A CLOCK... HANDS DOWN.

TENNIS IS ONE OF THE NOISIEST SPORTS TO WATCH BECAUSE EACH PLAYER RAISES A RACKET.

ON THE OTHER HAND, YOU HAVE DIFFERENT FINGERS.

I WANTED TO LEARN TO DRIVE STICK SHIFT, BUT I COULDN'T FIND A MANUAL.

REMAINS TO BE SEEN IF GLASS COFFINS BECOME POPULAR.

CONFUCIUS SAY, MAN WHO RUNS BEHIND CAR WILL GET EXHAUSTED, BUT MAN WHO RUNS IN FRONT OF CAR WILL GET TIRED.

I USED TO BE A BANKER, BUT THEN I LOST INTEREST.

DID YOU HEAR ABOUT THE SICK ITALIAN CHEF? UNFORTUNATELY, HE PASTAWAY.

THE FUTURE, THE PRESENT AND THE PAST WALKED INTO A BAR. THINGS GOT A LITTLE TENSE.

THIS MAY BE
CHEESY BUT I THINK
YOU'RE GRATE.

YOU AND I MAKE
A PERFECT MATCH.

R.I.P. BOILED WATER. YOU WILL BE MIST.

THIS GIRL SAID SHE RECOGNIZED ME FROM THE VEGETARIAN CLUB BUT I'VE NEVER SEEN HERBIVORE.

I OWE A LOT TO THE SIDEWALKS. THEY'VE BEEN KEEPING ME OFF THE STREETS FOR YEARS.

I USED TO BUILD STAIRS FOR A LIVING, IT'S AN UP AND DOWN BUSINESS.

I TRIED TO ESCAPE THE APPLE STORE. I COULDN'T BECAUSE THERE WERE NO WINDOWS.

DON'T TRUST PEOPLE THAT DO ACUPUNCTURE, THEY'RE BACK STABBERS.

WHEN IT CAME TO GETTING EVEN WITH MY LOCAL BUS COMPANY, I PULLED OUT ALL THE STOPS.

SEA CAPTAINS DON'T LIKE CREW CUTS.

TWO SILKWORMS HAD A RACE. THEY ENDED UP IN A TIE.

I TRIED TO BE A CHEF - FIGURED IT WOULD ADD A LITTLE SPICE TO MY LIFE, BUT I JUST DIDN'T HAVE THE THYME.

WHO CARES
WHEN I'M HURT.

I FEEL SAFE WHEN I'M WITH YOU.

HE BROKE INTO SONG WHEN HE COULDN'T FIND THE KEY.

A FRIEND OF MINE TRIED TO ANNOY ME WITH BIRD PUNS, BUT I SOON REALIZED THAT TOUCAN PLAY AT THAT GAME.

I THOUGHT ABOUT BECOMING A WITCH, SO I TRIED IT OUT FOR A SPELL.

I ACCIDENTALLY HANDED MY WIFE A GLUE STICK INSTEAD OF A CHAPSTICK. SHE STILL ISN'T TALKING TO ME.

A CARDBOARD BELT WOULD BE A WAIST OF PAPER.

THE FIRST TIME I GOT A UNIVERSAL REMOTE CONTROL, I THOUGHT TO MYSELF "THIS CHANGES EVERYTHING."

ONCE YOU HAVE SEEN ONE SHOPPING CENTER, YOU'VE SEEN A MALL.

I TRIED TO BE A TAILOR, BUT I WASN'T SUITED FOR IT... MAINLY BECAUSE IT WAS A SO-SO JOB.

TWO HATS WERE HANGING ON A HAT RACK IN THE HALLWAY. ONE HAT SAID TO THE OTHER, "YOU STAY HERE; I'LL GO ON A HEAD."

PENCILS COULD BE MADE WITH ERASERS AT BOTH ENDS, BUT WHAT WOULD BE THE POINT?

YOU MAKE A
VERY GOOD POINT.

YOU BLOW.
YOU SUCK.

MY FEAR OF MOVING STAIRS IS ESCALATING.

I BOUGHT A DICTIONARY AND WHEN I GOT HOME I REALIZED ALL THE PAGES WERE BLANK: I HAVE NO WORDS FOR HOW ANGRY I AM.

THREE CONSPIRACY THEORISTS WALK INTO A BAR. YOU CAN'T TELL ME THAT'S JUST A COINCIDENCE!

DON'T DRINK WITH GHOSTS, THEY CAN'T HANDLE THEIR BOOS.

POLICE WERE CALLED TO A DAYCARE CENTER WHERE A THREE-YEAR-OLD WAS RESISTING A REST.